'Off Duty'. This print is typical of many popular illustrations which romanticised the late Victorian sailor. The dashing young Commander courts his lady friend, somewhat incongruously draped over a machine gun! The warships in the background are 'dressed overall'.

THE VICTORIAN SAILOR

David Marc

Shire Publicat

CONTENTS

Set in 9 point Times roman and printed in Great Britain by C. I. Thomas & Sons (Haverfordwest) Ltd, Press Buildings, Merlins Bridge, Haverfordwest, Dyfed.

British Library Cataloguing in Publication data available.

ACKNOWLEDGEMENTS

The author offers special thanks to Susan Alvey, who produced the typescript, and Tony Holmes, who undertook the photographic work. The illustrations are from original photographs and negatives in the possession of the author or the University of Nottingham Centre for Local History.

COVER: *A group of seamen, circa 1860. This print shows an officer and four sailors' on board a merchant ship. The sailors' clothes adhere to broadly accepted conventions, and the officer puffs casually at a cigarette as he remonstrates with a crewman.*

A popular view of the sailor. This cartoon, printed in 1823, projects a popular view of the sailor as earnest but not very bright. Warned by his wife that no one must speak in church, Jack goes on to molest the parson for saying 'amen' and then initiating a 'mutiny' by inviting the congregation to sing a psalm. Sailors felt ill at ease with the conventions of landlubbers!

The Royal Navy. Lieutenant HRH Prince George, Duke of York, in command of Torpedo Boat Number 79 in 1889. The torpedo was one of the new weapons which was to revolutionise naval tactics in the late nineteenth century.

INTRODUCTION

During the reign of Queen Victoria Britain had the largest navy and mercantile marine that the world had ever seen, ships which traded with and policed an empire spread throughout the globe, and the sailors who manned these ships became almost folk heroes, the custodians of Nelson's tradition and the bringers of strange tales from across the seas. Authors, advertisers and artists all exploited the popularity of the sailor image, linked as it was with the active patronage of the royal family.

But often this has disguised the realities of the sailor's life. Separated from their homes and families for long periods, crowded below decks in skimpy living conditions and continually subjected to appalling dangers in the rigging of a rolling and pitching ship, sailors were familiar with discomfort and danger. But there was a lighter side to their life too, often displayed in a sense of comradeship which arose from shared privation and

danger: making a model below decks, singing a shanty to the accompaniment of a fiddler perched on the capstan or enjoying a wild 'run' ashore in San Francisco or Melbourne. These were times when the sailor could forget, for a while, the hardships of his life at sea.

This book examines the life of the Victorian sailor, in both the Royal Navy and the merchant service. The coming of steam power and iron and steel shipbuilding changed the sailor's life for the better in many ways, and some important reforms in the Royal Navy created a career structure for both officers and men for the first time. By the time of Queen Victoria's death in 1901 seafaring life had improved considerably, though many of the hazards and hardships still remained. Old seamen repeated the proverb 'Ships of wood, men of iron: ships of iron, men of wood'. For them, at least, it summed up the transition of the Victorian sailor.

3

ABOVE: *A shipwrecked sailor signals to a passing vessel with his jacket in an illustration from the children's novel 'Ellen Tremaine' by Marienne Filleul. Stirring tales of the sea were popular with young readers at least until the beginning of the First World War.*

ABOVE, LEFT: *Queen Victoria's eldest son, Edward, Prince of Wales, is portrayed in a sailor suit in this painting by Winterhalter. The costume is accurate to the smallest detail and later became popular with parents of much less exalted rank.*

LEFT: *'Players please.' The Nottingham firm of Players patented this famous design in 1891. The portrait was based on a real sailor, Thomas Huntley Wood, who later shaved off his beard to avoid repeated jokes and questions!*

This mezzotint, dated 1835, shows a sailor risking his life to save a woman and child from a raging sea during a shipwreck. Such motifs of the sailor hero were consistently popular with the Victorian public.

SAILORS IN ART, LITERATURE AND LEGEND

Victorian sailors enjoyed a unique relationship with their fellow countrymen which stemmed partly from the past and partly from the peculiar features of their own age. The British tar was closely linked with British greatness, a bond which went back at least to Trafalgar and which was strengthened by the creation of the colonial empire in the nineteenth century. Traditional virtues, it was believed, lay behind all of these achievements — courage, resourcefulness, devotion to duty — qualities which were epitomised in the sailor's life.

People were constantly being reminded of the idealised British sailor, sometimes in a form which embodied heroism, romance and mystery, as in the story of Sir John Franklin. Franklin, who disappeared in search of the North-west Passage in 1845, was the sailor hero *par excellence,* the man who made the supreme sacrifice for the greater glory of Britain. And it was not just high-ranking officers who were lionised in this way. In January 1873 the emigrant ship *Northfleet* was run down and sunk off Dungeness with huge loss of life. The captain and crew struggled manfully to avert disaster. Captain Knowles 'did his duty to the last like a brave British seaman' and his crew were described as 'true-hearted men . . . . striving to the last to save the weak and helpless ones around them'. Such stalwart qualities came to be expected.

The status of the sailor was further improved by the active support of the royal family and the publicity brought by successful overseas warfare. War brought further opportunities for heroism — the Victoria Cross awarded to Joseph Trewavis in 1855, for example — and the exploits of the Naval Brigades before Sebastopol and Ladysmith were much publicised. Following in the footsteps of her uncle the 'sailor King', William IV,

5

Victoria's second son, Prince Alfred, joined the navy as did her grandson Prince George, later King George V. The fleet reviews helped convert this royal patronage into more broad-based enthusiasm. About six hundred thousand people witnessed the Spithead Review of 1856, a number which was greatly surpassed by the Jubilee Reviews of 1887 and 1897. By then the sailor suit had become a popular form of dress for children, and people of all classes included visits to warships as part of a good holiday by the sea, now for the first time made possible by the advent of the railways.

Ships also stood at the forefront of technical development. Experimental steamers such as the *Great Eastern* and the *Great Britain* received wide publicity, because of their hugeness or mechanical innovation. The men who put to sea in these vessels were not only pioneers of a technological revolution, but they were also the best link with strange and mysterious lands across the seas which most people had only heard about. The sailor who stepped off some snorting and puffing steamship with a parrot on his arm

was every schoolboy's hero, rather like the astronaut today. The Victorian age was one of broadening horizons, but also of naive curiosity, and the sailor satisfied both of these requirements.

How did all of this affect the lives of landsmen? How was the image of the sailor projected? The most pervasive influence was probably books about the sea. The classic novels *Treasure Island* and *Robinson Crusoe* have obvious maritime overtones, and popular children's authors, such as R. M. Ballantyne and W. H. G. Kingston, sought to improve the moral fibre of their youthful readers with stirring tales of the sea. But the outstanding maritime author of the age was Joseph Conrad. A Pole by birth, Conrad was a naturalised Briton who rose to be a captain in the merchant service; after his retirement in 1893 at the age of thirty-six he devoted his time to writing, and his unique perception of the late Victorian sailor is based on personal experience. His best novels are set at sea and examine the contrasting personalities of a ship's crew under the stress of bad weather. Conrad's seamen are not the

'Sailor's Return'. This Sunderland ware jug of around 1830 depicts three sailors carousing with women after their return from sea. The reverse is decorated with a sentimental poem about the sailor's life.

cardboard cut-outs of newspaper reports or popular fiction: not all are heroes, but the impression is conveyed that they were mostly good and brave men, like the old shellback Singleton, the quiet hero of *The Nigger of the Narcissus*.

Even for the many Victorians who did not read books, it was still difficult to escape from the sailor image. The comic operas of Gilbert and Sullivan often used maritime motifs, notably in *HMS Pinafore*, and for a less highbrow audience there were the melodramatic performances of the sailor/actor T. P. Cooke in popular plays such as *Black Ey'd Susan*. Advertisers, too, soon exploited the popularity of sailors. Tobacco companies were especially keen on the navy connection, the most famous example being the sailor and lifebelt design registered by Players in 1891: the golden sunset and the firm purposeful face of the bearded sailor carried a special message to the Victorian public.

The home, too, was likely to be invaded by nautical images. Seascapes by dynasties of artists such as the Carmichaels and the Knells were popular drawing-room pictures for the expanding middle class, and mass-produced prints served the same purpose lower down the social scale. The Staffordshire potteries manufactured flatback figures of Admirals Napier and Dundas, as well as the elusive Sir John Franklin. The potteries of Wearside and the glassworks of Bristol and Nailsea all manufactured domestic ephemera — jugs, bowls, rolling pins — festooned with pictures of ships or sentimental motifs such as 'The Sailor's Return' or 'The Sailor's Farewell'. Sailors had become good business, as well as being an embodiment of nationalistic pride.

ABOVE: *Following in father's footsteps? A small boy from Hull wearing the ubiquitous 'sailor suit' and clutching a toy boat. The picture illustrates well the potent appeal of the sea amongst the Victorian public.*

BELOW: *HMS 'Northumberland', built in 1798, is depicted on this blue glass rolling pin, made around 1830. These rolling pins were regarded as good luck charms both by sailors and by their friends and families at home.*

ABOVE: *Steamships did much to improve the life of Victorian sailors. Here is a typical example, the 'Zoe' built at Whitby in 1878. She was eventually stranded off the coast of Brazil in 1887 with the loss of two of her crew.*

LEFT: *A chief engineer of about 1900. The men who looked after the engines of the new steamers were an increasingly important breed. Social acceptance was slower. 'Oil and water don't mix', said some of the older deck officers.*

A training ship medal of about 1900, awarded to J. E. Glover AB for eighteen months' sea service with good conduct. He was a trainee on the 'Arethusa', an ex-navy frigate moored at Greenhithe. The 'Arethusa', which was supposed to prepare destitute boys for a life at sea, was patronised by the great Victorian philanthropist Baroness Burdett-Coutts (1814-1907).

LIFE IN THE MERCHANT SERVICE

The Victorian age saw a revolution in merchant shipping. By the middle of the century the square-built sailing ship, characteristic of the eighteenth century, was giving way to the more graceful lines of the clipper, and by 1900 huge iron and steel 'down-easters' dominated those ocean routes still plied by sail. But steam power was perhaps the most important innovation. Although still experimental in the 1840s, the steam compound engine was perfected by the 1860s and the more efficient triple expansion engine by the 1880s. It was this last development that finally guaranteed the superiority of steam over sail on most ocean routes, and Britain's trade routes spanned the globe. British sailors brought nitrate, guano and copper ore from South America, wool from Australia and New Zealand, and tea from China: emigration to North America and Australia provided further busi-ness, as did the supply of coaling stations to fuel the new steamers. Other sailors found employment in coastal trades or in specialist ventures such as sealing and whaling.

Life for officers in the merchant service could be good. All ships carried a master and a range of mates who were responsi-ble for the navigation and general man-agement of the ship. In earlier times many officers had graduated from the lower deck, but after 1850 they in-creasingly obtained their positions by Board of Trade certification. Moreover, premiums were payable by apprentices, and so a growing gulf emerged between officers and men in the merchant service. Officers enjoyed relatively comfortable accommodation and many had the pri-vilege of taking their wives and children to sea. Master mariners, in particular, could earn considerable sums by virtue of

LEFT: *This engraving was published in 1838 and is entitled 'Signal for an Engagement — Home'. The sailor's costume is typical of the era, comprising tight trousers, a striped shirt and monkey jacket; these must have been shoregoing clothes, since work would have been difficult in such restrictive garments.*

RIGHT: *Sailor's uniform, about 1875. The short jacket and bell-bottomed tousers were widely used by sailors in both the Royal Navy and the merchant service. Note also the broad-brimmed hat which was more decorative than functional.*

their wages and a manipulation of their positions of authority.

Beneath the officers, the seamen had a hierarchy of their own. At the top of the scale came the so called 'idlers', the bosun, carpenter, sailmaker and cook, who had specific responsibilities, did not keep watches and received higher wages. Most numerous, however, were the able seamen and ordinary seamen, who had to do the majority of the work. Many nationalities were represented in the fo'c'sle of a typical merchantman and towards the end of the nineteenth century non-British seamen became more common in sail as many of their British counterparts opted for safer and more comfortable berths in steamships.

Conditions at sea could be arduous, especially under sail. Sailors generally lived in the fo'c'sle or in a deckhouse, having a narrow bunk or hammock to sleep in and a sea chest for their personal belongings: accommodation was cramped and subject to the extremes of climate. Minimum standards of food were laid down by the Merchant Shipping Acts. It comprised such items as 'pantiles' (ship's biscuits) and 'salt horse' (salted beef or pork): additional items could sometimes be purchased from benevolent shipowners, but at a price. The working day at sea was divided into 'watches' of four hours followed by four hours of rest, a routine which continued seven days a week: thus, the sailor worked a minimum of eighty four hours per week, and more if weather conditions were bad.

Watches were divided by a system of bells which comprised the sailor's clock. Watches commenced at midnight, so the watch changed at four o'clock and eight

ABOVE: *The officers' saloon on the 'Cutty Sark' was relatively comfortable and well appointed. The panelling was of teak and bird's-eye maple and some of the seating, at least, was comfortably upholstered.*

BELOW: *Some tools of the trade. Top, a fid for splicing rope; centre, a Royal Navy 'bosun's call' for piping officers aboard; below, a knife with its sheath; right, sailmaker's palm and needle for stitching canvas.*

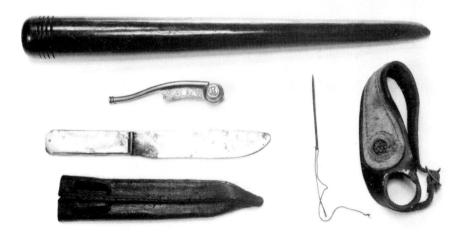

ABOVE: *Taking in sail in heavy weather. The four sailors on the foreyard are securing the mainsail to prevent it blowing away in the severe weather. A big wave has just broken over the starboard gunwale. The dangers of working aloft in these conditions are obvious.*

BELOW: *Steering in a heavy swell. The officer of the watch keeps an eye on the compass while two sailors look after the wheel. An extra hand was needed in these conditions to guard against the violent kicking of the rudder, which could cause serious injury to the helmsman.*

Preparing for the kill. A harpooner on the deck of a whaler uses a fid to attach the foreganger to his harpoon. Despite the romanticism of whaling in popular songs and literature, it was a cruel and sordid business.

o'clock in the morning, twelve noon and so on. The only exceptions to this rule were the two short 'dog watches', each of two hours duration, which lasted between four in the afternoon and eight in the evening. The first half-hour of a new watch was indicated by a single chime on the ship's bell, and at the end of an hour the bell was rung twice. Thus by the end of a normal watch eight bells were chimed, signifying that it was time for the crew roster to change. The bell was always rung in couples and singles. Three bells, for example, would be rendered by two rings in rapid succession followed after a pause by a third, rather than by three evenly spaced chimes.

The sailor's work was varied. Steering by the compass, splicing rope and working with the sails and rigging required specialist knowledge as well as courage to perform tasks as much as 150 feet (46 m) above the deck. Many duties, on the other hand, were more mechanical: holystoning the decks, chipping rust or working the capstan. Because many of these skills were not readily reusable on land it was difficult for a sailor to give up the seafaring life, even if he had had enough of its dangers and privation.

Dangers, indeed, were manifold, both to ships and to individuals. Ships foundered in heavy weather, collided in crowded estuaries, ran aground as a result of navigational errors or were burned to the water line by the spontaneous ignition of dangerous cargoes. Indeed, many ships were deliberately sent to sea in an unsafe condition or were sunk in order to collect the insurance premiums on their cargoes. In all of this it was the sailor who was the loser. Between 1879 and 1899 1153 British ships went missing and almost eleven thousand lives were lost. Hazards to the individual were almost as alarming. Falls from the

13

aptly described by Herman Melville as 'land sharks'. These men, who gloried in names such as Calico Jim and Shanghai Kelly, tempted seamen ashore into bars and brothels and then plied them with drink or drugs until they were senseless. When they woke up, their money would invariably have been stolen and they would find themselves aboard some out-ward-bound vessel, the crimp having 'sold' them to the master for an advance on their wages. This process, known as 'shanghaiing', was an accepted part of life in most of the world's seaports.

Only the activities of benevolent in-stitutions, such as the Missions to Seamen and the Liverpool Sailors' Home, pro-vided an alternative to the dangers of the dockside ghetto. The chaplains of the Missions to Seamen, known to genera-tions of sailors as the 'Flying Angel', would board vessels as they came into port and introduce themselves to the master; then they would mingle with the crew dispensing bibles and solace where appropriate. Many sailors had reserva-tions about this, but there were also hostels ashore which they could visit, providing recreation and companionship. These were at least cleaner and safer than many of their customary haunts.

There was, however, a lighter side to life, and recreations such as shark fishing or hunting albatrosses amused many sailors, despite the taboos of Coleridge's *Ancient Mariner*. Ceremonies such as 'crossing the line' or 'selling the dead horse' provided opportunities to dress up or to have fun, and music and dancing were always important pastimes. Music aboard ship fell into two categories. On the one hand there was music made by sailors for entertainment, the singing of folk songs in the fo'c'sle or performances by impromptu 'foo-foo' bands. On the other hand there were shanties, which were basically work songs related to hauling and heaving and designed to coordinate muscular effort as well as reducing the tedium of the task. A shantyman could usually be sure of a good berth on account of his talents, and this was shrewd business for captains and shipowners: 'a good shantyman's worth six more hands on the rope', it was often said.

Heaving the log. The log measured the speed of the ship through the water, its line being divided by knots. The officer holds an hourglass to allow the log to run out for fourteen seconds.

rigging or blows from swinging blocks and spars accounted for many deaths and serious injuries. American ships had a particularly bad reputation for the vio-lence of some of their masters and 'bucko' mates, who used belaying pins and the knotted ends of ropes to extract maximum effort from their crews. One notorious character, 'Bully' Waterman, used to amuse himself by shooting at men in the rigging and was finally brought to trial, but acquitted, for the murder of an Italian seaman.

After a long spell at sea sailors looked forward to a 'run' ashore in one of the dockside areas such as San Francisco's 'Barbary Coast' or London's 'Tiger Bay'. These places provided drink, music halls and prostitutes but were dominated by the sinister crimps and boarding masters,

ABOVE: *Repair work at sea. Watched by a boy, a sailor repairs a sail on the poop of the 'Cutty Sark' in 1886. A large seabird, possibly an albatross, sits in the foreground.*

BELOW: *A gale in the Caribbean. The transport ship 'Herefordshire', carrying the 7th Royal Fusiliers, overtaken by a gale in the Gulf of Florida in 1848. Sailors can be seen undertaking the dangerous job of lowering the topmasts and yards in order to reduce the top weight of the vessel: officers shout orders from the deck.*

ABOVE: *A sailing ship, stranded off the Lizard, being broken up by heavy seas; the foremast is about to fall. Shipwrecks such as this accounted for thousands of lost lives.*

BELOW: *A group of guests, mostly female, on board the 'Cutty Sark' at Sydney in 1887. The ship's officers and apprentices all wear uniform except Captain Woodget and Jerry Dimint, the mate (centre, left) both of whom are distinguished by unusual hats. Female company was always welcome after a long trip.*

The introduction of breech-loading guns, to replace the old muzzle loaders, was a major technological development and a naval school of gunnery was established aboard HMS 'Excellent'. In this picture, from about 1890, a group of sailors are firing a ten inch gun under the supervision of an officer.

LIFE IN THE ROYAL NAVY

The revolution in ship design was greater in the Royal Navy than in the merchant service because, in addition to the sailing qualities of a vessel, its armament had to be considered too. In 1837 the majority of ships were still Nelsonian in appearance and there were only a few experimental steamers noted in the *Navy List,* with arguments between the exponents of screw propulsion and supporters of the paddle. In the 1840s the first paddle frigates were built and both old and new wooden warships began to be fitted with auxiliary steam power. However, it was the launch of HMS *Warrior* in 1860 that heralded the real breakthrough. Thereafter the purpose-built 'ironclad' became the most important naval vessel, and in the 1870s and 1880s many experimental designs were tried before the perfection of the classic 'pre-*Dreadnought*' battleship of the 1890s.

There was only one major war during this period, in the Crimea (1854-6), and during it the navy undertook operations in the Baltic and the Black Sea. Minor

colonial wars were more frequent and the navy was engaged in many of these as well as sometimes providing men to fight ashore in Naval Brigades. But conflict was not the main purpose of Victoria's navy, for there were no major enemies left to defeat. More important was the policing of the *Pax Britannica*, guaranteeing that the world's trade routes were free and safe from hazard. This involved the navy in important tasks such as polar exploration, the drawing up of charts and the suppression of piracy, slaving and smuggling.

This new navy was served by a rapidly changing body of men. In 1837 most of the officers still came from wealthy families, undertook their training at sea and relied largely on influence and patronage for their promotion up to the rank of captain. Beyond that advancement became a cause of grievance because it was based entirely on seniority, not merit, and the huge redundancies of officers after 1815 meant that the system was clogged: promotion in the navy was literally a matter of waiting to step into

LEFT: *Naval officers at the beginning of Victoria's reign still resembled their predecessors of the Nelsonian era. This officer (a lieutenant) wears only one epaulette on his right shoulder in accordance with uniform regulations in force between 1812 and 1846.*

RIGHT: *Greenwich pensioners. Greenwich Hospital was founded in 1694 for infirm and disabled seamen. During Victoria's reign wounded veterans of the Napoleonic Wars were a common sight, and at times over two thousand were resident in or near the Hospital. Many more roamed the streets with little proper sustenance.*

dead men's shoes. There was also a rift between those officers who held the Queen's Commission and those who merely held Navy Office warrants — masters, mates, surgeons and pursers. Despite the important contribution they made to the navigation, health and administration of the ship they tended to be looked down on by their commissioned colleagues.

Like the officers, most seamen entered as volunteers, often encouraged by the payment of a 'prest' or bounty, and undertook their training at sea. The press gang, though still legal, was not used after 1815. Few sailors could have regarded the navy as a career since they were engaged for one commission only. On the lower deck many grievances had

remained unaltered since the great naval mutinies of 1797. Sailors still complained of bad and irregular pay, poor conditions and the extensive use of flogging by many captains. Keel hauling had long been discredited as a punishment at sea, but rumours circulated that sadistic captains still occasionally enforced it: it could amount to a death sentence on the unfortunate sailor on whom it was inflicted.

To its credit, Victoria's government did not neglect these grievances. In 1847 and 1851 steps were taken to relieve the blockage in the *Navy List* by retiring large numbers of senior officers. Thereafter, compulsory retirement at the age of fifty-five or sixty ensured that the problem would not recur. In 1857 a new

ABOVE: *Dead men's shoes. The Waiting Room at the Admiralty in the early nineteenth century was where officers gathered in search of preferment. It often proved to be a long wait followed by disappointment.*
BELOW: *These sailors pictured aboard HMS 'Phoebe' in 1864 are wearing the new uniform for ratings introduced in 1857. Bare feet were still the order of the day to maximise grip on the wooden decks.*

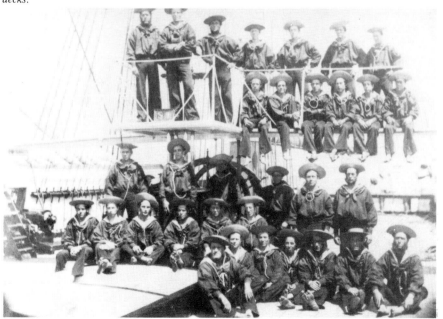

ABOVE: *Living quarters in the Royal Navy. Sailors lived, ate and slept around the guns which they manned in battle. Hammocks, storage utensils and a makeshift table and benches can be seen in this picture. All of these quickly disappeared when a ship was 'cleared for action'.*

BELOW: *The gundeck of a warship around 1835. Sailors in the Royal Navy undertook their recreation on the gundeck, and this print shows a scene in port with women in evidence for dancing and other activities. Shore leave was generally forbidden for fear of desertion. Note the lack of uniform at this period.*

ABOVE: *A midshipmen's mess, about 1840. Midshipmen generally messed in the gun-room on warships and the gunner took care of their clothing and food. They often engaged in high jinks and horseplay as this print shows. Many items of equipment are illustrated here including an octant, a loud hailer and a dirk.*

BELOW, LEFT: *George E. Cave aged about fifteen (around 1882), a cadet and later Midshipman aboard HMS 'Temeraire'. After 1858 officer cadets were first sent for a spell of training on board the old three-decker HMS 'Britannia' before being drafted to seagoing ships. The training of naval officers improved markedly during Victoria's reign.*

BELOW, RIGHT: *The Baltic Medal, awarded to sailors for service in the Baltic, 1854-5. This example bears the name of Charles H. Pender who served aboard HMS 'Leopard', an early paddle frigate and flagship to the squadron.*

LEFT: *A petty officer, photographed around 1880, with a 'full set' (beard and moustache), epitomises the 'navy look' fashionable amongst seafarers in the late nineteenth century, not least the future King George V. The wearing of beards and moustaches was sanctioned in 1869.*

RIGHT: *An able seaman, photographed around 1890, wearing the uniform typical of the late Victorian period. Unlike army uniform, it has changed little since then. The cap tally bears the name of Nelson's 'Victory', which until 1922 was flagship of the Portsmouth Command.*

scheme was introduced for the education and examination of naval cadets and midshipmen. This involved training at sea and aboard HMS *Britannia* at Dartmouth, and at the age of nineteen midshipmen were allowed to sit examinations to obtain the ranks of sub-lieutenant and lieutenant. There was also more scope for a new officer entrant to specialise. In 1843 the senior warrant officers received commissions and in 1847 engineers received wardroom status. This was a considerable reform considering the prejudice against the steam engine amongst many traditionally minded officers.

For the seamen the most important innovation was the principle of con-tinuous service. This had its origins as far back as 1830, but in 1853 it was decided that all boy entrants should be engaged for at least ten years after the age of eighteen. For the first time this provided the possibility of a career in the navy and training was improved accordingly. Like the officers, lower-deck entrants spent a period aboard a training ship, such as HMS *Ganges* at Falmouth, and also had a spell of practical experience at sea. At the age of eighteen the trainee would be rated as ordinary seaman and thereafter was able to climb a ladder of promotion through the ranks of able seaman and leading seaman up to petty officer and chief petty officer rank. There was scope

ABOVE: *The foredeck of a battleship, about 1895. A petty officer poses beneath the 13.5 inch guns of a battleship of the 'Royal Sovereign' class, identified by her barbettes (gun mountings) and twin funnels sitting side by side. The sailors are in tropical rig and the immaculate deck and superstructure is a testimony to their hard work.*

BELOW: *A contemporary photograph to that above; sailors, organised in watches, undertaking cutlass drill under the watchful eye of their officers (wearing swords). The exercise is taking place on the quarter-deck of a battleship of the 'Royal Sovereign' class.*

ABOVE: *A ship's crew in coaling, around 1900. Coaling ship was one of the most dirty and backbreaking tasks undertaken by sailors in the Royal Navy. It involved carrying innumerable sacks of coal from colliers or shore dumps into the ship's bunkers. Traditionally the whole ship's company shared in the task.*

BELOW: *A foo-foo band at the end of the nineteenth century. Recreation aboard ship was such as could be improvised and provided by the men themselves. The sailors with the mandolin and flute provided accompaniment while the others sang for the entertainment of their shipmates.*

HMS 'Powerful', a cruiser built in 1895 and armed with two 9.2 inch guns, twelve 6 inch guns, and sixteen twelve-pounders. She was typical of many late Victorian ships designed to police an expanding Empire. On this postcard illustration her crew is seen lining the deck while the huge flags give a suitably patriotic flavour to the design.

for specialism on the lower deck too. Some entrants became signalmen, others attended special courses on gunnery or torpedoes. These developments were paralleled by a similar career structure for engine-room staff.

Conditions on board a warship were still overcrowded and harsh, with all social life centred on the damp, dark and stinking gundecks, but at least there were some improvements which helped to make life more tolerable. Pay was increased and in 1851 an allotment scheme was introduced enabling sailors to send regular payments to their wives and families at home. The standard of food was improved and there were moves to phase out the brain-numbing issues of 'grog' in favour of more fresh water, tea and cocoa. Uniform was introduced for ratings in 1857, replacing the 'slops' sold by the purser, and medals for campaigns and long service and good conduct helped

foster an *esprit de corps* on the lower deck. Flogging was suspended in peacetime in 1871 and during wartime in 1879.

By the late nineteenth century it was evident that the navy was attracting a better class of recruit and there was no problem in keeping well manned ships at sea in peacetime. Indeed, war was no longer regarded with the trepidation that it used to be, owing to the establishment of the Royal Naval Reserve in 1858. This organisation drew officers and men from the merchant service, trained them and made them liable for naval service in the event of war: by 1862 twelve thousand men had enrolled. Victoria's navy certainly lacked the corruption and cruelty of Nelson's era but perhaps it had also lost some of its romance and heroism: by becoming more professional the navy had become less individualistic and it was on this sort of eccentric flair that the 'Nelson touch' had been based.

ABOVE: *Many sailors passed the time by painting pictures of their ships in a distinctive 'primitive' style. Sometimes these pictures were fixed to the tops of their sea chests as a form of decoration. This example has written on the back of the canvas 'Ship, Henry Reed, 1868'.*

BELOW: *Another form of folk art was the diorama. This involved placing a half model of the ship in front of a background which often showed a coastline and features such as a lighthouse. This shows the 'Henrietta', built around 1860, and epitomises the changes of the mid-Victorian period. Her hull is still painted in 'Nelson chequer', but alongside her steams a small paddle tug, symbol of a new age.*

Model making at sea; two sailors have brought their models on deck during a spell of fine weather. The larger model is a barque, possibly a representation of the ship the men are travelling on. The smaller one is destined for a bottle. Note the carrying device, and the rigging threads attached to the central spindle: this was to re-erect the masts and rigging after they had been collapsed to pass through the neck of the bottle.

SAILORS' HANDICRAFTS

Handicrafts were an important part of the sailor's life and surviving examples provide the only tangible link with a long vanished generation of men. This important form of folk art can still be viewed in many museums and collections, though the work of fakers has made it difficult to distinguish original pieces from counterfeits.

In the nineteenth century ships were manned for 'maximum intensity', which was both essential and cheap in an age when wages were low. A warship had to carry enough crew to man the guns in battle; a clipper needed enough manpower to take her around Cape Horn in the worst imaginable conditions. But for the vast majority of the time not all of this workforce was needed: ships were overmanned, though the problem was greater on sailing ships than on steamers.

On almost all vessels some time was given over to handicraft. There was little else to do. Many sailors were illiterate and on a long voyage the possibilities of conversation became quickly exhausted: drink was generally banned or strictly limited. Indeed, some captains seem to have encouraged their men to have hobbies, perhaps because they saw in them an antidote to the discontent which was always endemic at sea.

The scale and quality of sailors' output must be linked to the difficulties in which they lived and worked. Modelling was difficult in the cramped conditions below decks and it was made worse by the constant movement of the ship. Tools and materials were also difficult to come by: the modeller either went to sea

prepared or made the best of what he could find lying around.

Makers of ships in bottles generally had a set of special instruments, which they took from ship to ship and kept in the ditty box of their sea chest or kit bag. Others depended on such everyday tools as a sharp knife for cutting and carving and a sailmaker's needle for more intricate scratch work. Materials were generally whatever could be stolen or

LEFT: *Sailors' dolls. One form of handicraft aboard ship was making dolls out of scrap pieces of turned wooden oars or spars. These could then be given as presents to wives or children at home.*

BELOW: *The sailor's farewell. This woolwork picture of about 1860 shows a sailor taking leave of his wife or sweetheart before returning to his ship. Two shipmates wait for him, having taken off their shoregoing jackets in anticipation of a long haul. The ship offshore is HMS 'Emerald', a wooden fifty-one gun frigate built in 1856. Such sentimental motifs were common in sailors' handicrafts.*

28

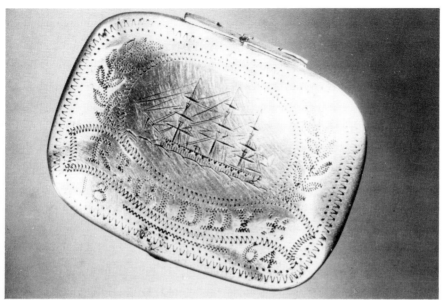

A sailor's tobacco box. This small brass box, designed to take tobacco or snuff, was skilfully decorated by its sailor owner. It depicts an early ironclad very similar to HMS 'Warrior' and bears the name of Robert Giddy and the date 1864.

scrounged: a lick of paint from the fo'c'sle store, a lump of wood from the cargo battens or a vandalised tobacco tin.

Creative ideas stemmed from a range of inspirations, chief of which was the ship itself. Walking ashore, in shipping offices or dockside pubs, sailors saw professionally executed builder's models and half models and came back determined to try something similar themselves. The appeal of the ship image was universal amongst seafarers. Captains and mates could afford to commission paintings by professional 'pierhead artists', but on the lower deck sailors had to trust in their own skills and they often learned considerably from one another. Indeed, the emulative element is extremely strong in nautical handicraft, a feature well illustrated by the spate of woolwork pictures, which were popular in the Royal Navy in the second half of the nineteenth century.

One of the best known forms of nautical handicraft is the bone 'prisoner-of-war' model, so called because they were first made by French prisoners captured during the Napoleonic Wars. Many of these men had specialist technical skills and whiled away the hours of captivity by making extraordinarily detailed models of warships for sale to curious visitors. One major centre of this work was the prison camp at Norman Cross, near Peterborough. Bone modelling survived the armistice of 1815. Some Frenchmen stayed in England to continue the craft, copies were made throughout the nineteenth century and some English sailors took up the hobby with enthusiasm. Modelling in wood was even more popular, because it did not present the technical difficulties encountered by the bone modeller. Many sailors built wooden models of their ships, often displaying a particular interest in the aspect of her tackle with which they were most familiar. Thus a topman would pay careful attention to the yards and rigging, whilst a gunner might show special interest in the vessel's armament.

If inspiration did not come from the ship or shipmates the sailor's imagination might have been fired by something which reminded him of home — his wife, children or sweetheart. Such sentimental motifs were particularly popular in scrimshaw work. Scrimshaw involved softening a whale's tooth or walrus tusk in brine and then engraving a decoration, like a tattoo, with a sharp needle. The lines would then be rubbed with a mixture of black ink and soot so that they would stand out boldly against the white background. Scrimshaw teeth are as often decorated with female figures as with whaling scenes; embroideries depict homecomings and farewells as well as pictures of ships at sea. Objects made on board ship could often have a practical use as presents for relatives and friends on shore, such as pie cutters, needlework tools and walking sticks.

The quality of this output varied greatly. At best it was very good but at the other extreme it could be appalling. The survival rate has fluctuated accordingly.

These artefacts were not much esteemed by society and the sailors themselves regarded them as a form of therapy, to be renewed on each voyage, rather than an art form which would stand the test of time. Once ashore, models and other examples of handicraft were often treated with scant respect. They might have been given to a captain or mate in return for some small favour or left carelessly at a lodging house in lieu of rent. And those models which were given to small children as a toy or novelty often disappeared without trace.

It was only in retirement, when many sailors continued their hobbies outside the back door in summer or before the hearth in winter, that models and embroideries were displayed with any permanence or pride. Old age and retirement provided a stability which sailors never had in their working lives.

GLOSSARY OF NAUTICAL WORDS AND EXPRESSIONS

Barque: three-masted sailing vessel square-rigged on the two forward masts.

Belaying pin: removable metal or wooden pin set in a rail to which ropes are secured.

Bells: system of timekeeping at sea.

Boarding master: a type of *crimp*.

Bosun: foreman of the sailors aboard a merchant ship, generally responsible for their work and discipline.

Bosun's call: distinctive metal whistle used in the Royal Navy to convey orders or 'pipe' officers aboard.

Bucko: tough or arbitrary (American slang).

Cleared for action: of the gundecks of a warship, rapidly cleared of 'domestic' obstacles before going into battle.

Clipper: fast sailing vessel typical of the 1850s and 1860s.

Crimp: agent who organises the provision of sailors for ship's captains.

Crossing the line: ceremony employed on crossing the equator. Novice members of the crew are subjected to special rites by an older sailor dressed as 'King Neptune'.

Ditty box: small enclosed section of a sea chest in which small or precious articles could be kept.

Dog watch: short two-hour watch at sea.

Down-easter: type of sailing vessel originating from the 'Down East' states of New England, USA.

Dressed overall: of a vessel decorated with signal flags and bunting, generally to celebrate some great event.

Fid: wooden pin used for splicing or repairing rope; a marlingspike was used to do the same job on wire.

Fo'c'sle: the foreward section of a ship often used for the stowage of tackle or accommodation of the crew.

Foo-foo band: improvised band, often with strange and ingenious instruments, got together for entertainment at sea.

Grog: daily ration of rum diluted with water, distributed in the Royal Navy from the mid eighteenth century but now discontinued.

Gun room: compartment in a warship used as a mess by the midshipmen.

Gunwale: bulwark constructed around the main deck of a vessel.

Holystone: block of soft sandstone used to scour wooden decks, giving a clean white appearance.

Idlers: petty officers aboard a merchant ship. So called because they did not keep watches and might have been regarded by the rest of the crew as having an easy life.

Ironclad: wooden-hulled ship protected by the addition of iron plates; an early form of armour.

Keel hauling: illegal punishment by which offenders, tied to a rope, were passed beneath the keel of a ship at sea. It could result in death or serious injury.

Log: metal object trailed astern of a ship to assess her speed in knots through the water.

Navy Office warrant: document, issued by the Navy Office, by which 'warrant officers' were appointed. Considered inferior to the Queen's Commission.

Nelson chequer: black and white pattern on the side of ships. In the navy it indicated gun ports, and in the merchant service false gun ports to deter pirates. Still used in the late nineteenth century.

Pantiles: nickname given to ship's biscuits, often hard and infested by weevils.

Poop: aftermost deck of ship often used for steering and navigation.

Press gang: means of compelling men to join the navy, often by removing them by armed force. Legal, but very unpopular.

Prest: payment made to induce men to volunteer for service in the navy.

Purser: warrant officer in the Royal Navy responsible for keeping accounts and the provision of food and clothing for the crew.

Queen's Commission: letters of authority, signed by the monarch, appointing officers in the navy.

Salt horse: nickname for salt beef and pork, though it might often have been horsemeat, as sailors suggested it was!

Scrimshaw: decoration of bone or ivory with engraved motifs. Pejorative word (in origin) which implies timewasting.

Selling the dead horse: after a month at sea a symbolic wooden horse was often pitched into the water. This symbolised the end of the period in which sailors in practice worked for nothing, since the first month's wage was often pledged to a crimp or agent.

Shanghaiing: practice, employed by crimps, of getting a man drunk in order to put him aboard an outward bound vessel.

Shanty: sailor's song sung while heaving and pulling. Often divided between solo sections, sung by a shantyman, and a chorus to which the whole crew contributes.

Shellback: old sailor.

Slops: cheap clothing sold to sailors by the purser aboard naval vessels before the introduction of uniforms.

Wardroom: mess for commissioned officers aboard a warship.

FURTHER READING

Archibald, E. *The Wooden Fighting Ship, 897-1860.* Blandford, 1968.
Archibald, E. *The Metal Fighting Ship, 1860-1970.* Blandford, 1971.
Banks, S. *The Handicrafts of the Sailor.* David and Charles, 1974.
Baynham, M. *Before the Mast.* Arrow, 1972.
Conrad, J. *The Nigger of the Narcissus.* Dent, 1963 (First published 1897).
Credland, A. G. *Whales and Whaling.* Shire Publications, 1982.
Dana, R. H. *Two Years before the Mast.* Milner and Company, 1840.
Greenhill, B., and Stonham, D. *Seafaring under Sail.* Patrick Stephens, 1981.
Kennedy, P. M. *The Rise and Fall of British Naval Mastery.* Allen Lane, 1976.
Lewis, M. *The Navy in Transition.* Hodder and Stoughton, 1965.
Rasor, E. L. *Reform in the Royal Navy, 1850-80.* Hamden, 1976.
White, C. *The End of the Sailing Navy.* Kenneth Mason, 1981.
Winton, J. *Hurrah for the Life of a Sailor.* Joseph, 1977.

PLACES TO VISIT

Intending visitors are advised to find out the times of opening before making a special journey.

Bucklers Hard Maritime Museum, Bucklers Hard, Beaulieu, Brockenhurst, Hampshire. Telephone: Bucklers Hard (059 063) 203.

Castle Cornet, St Peter Port, Guernsey, Channel Isles. Telephone: Guernsey (0481) 21657.

Cutty Sark Clipper Ship, King William Walk, Greenwich, London SE10 9BG. Telephone: 01-858 3445.

Exeter Maritime Museum, Isca Ltd, The Quay, Exeter, Devon EX2 4AN. Telephone: Exeter (0392) 58075.

Glasgow Museum of Transport, 25 Albert Drive, Glasgow G41 2PE. Telephone: 041-423 8000.

HMS Victory, HM Naval Base, Portsmouth, Hampshire PO1 3PZ. Telephone: Portsmouth (0705) 822351, extension 23111.

HMS Warrior, Coal Dock, Hartlepool, Cleveland. Telephone: Hartlepool (0429) 33051 or 67037. The ship may be visited at Hartlepool in 1985 and in 1986 will be moving to Portsmouth.

Maritime Museum for East Anglia, Marine Parade, Great Yarmouth, Norfolk. Telephone: Great Yarmouth (0493) 2267.

Merseyside Maritime Museum, Pier Head, Liverpool L12 0HB. Telephone: 051-228 5311.

Museum of Nautical Art, Chapel Street, Penzance, Cornwall TR18 4AF. Telephone: Penzance (0736) 3448.

Museum of Science and Engineering, Blandford House, West Blandford Street, Newcastle upon Tyne NE1 4HZ. Telephone: Newcastle upon Tyne (0632) 326789.

National Maritime Museum, Romney Road, Greenwich, London SE10 9NF. Telephone: 01-858 4422.

North Devon Maritime Museum, Odun House, Odun Road, Appledore, Bideford, Devon EX39 1PT. Telephone: Bideford (023 72) 6042.

Poole Maritime Museum, Paradise Street, The Quay, Poole, Dorset. Telephone: Poole (0202) 675151.

Royal Naval Museum, HM Naval Base, Portsmouth, Hampshire PO1 3LR. Telephone: Portsmouth (0705) 822351, extension 23868.

Science Museum, Exhibition Road, South Kensington, London SW7 2DD. Telephone: 01-589 3456.

Shipwreck Centre, Charlestown, Cornwall. | Telephone: St Austell (0726) 3331 or 3332.

SS Great Britain, Great Western Dock, Gas Ferry Road, Bristol BS1 6TY. Telephone: Bristol (0272) 20680.

Swansea Maritime and Industrial Museum, South Dock, Swansea, West Glamorgan. Telephone: Swansea (0792) 50351.

Town Docks Museum, Queen Victoria Square, Hull, North Humberside HU1 3DX. Telephone: Hull (0482) 222737.

Valhalla Maritime Museum, Tresco Abbey, Tresco, Isles of Scilly TR24 0QQ. Telephone: Scillonia (0720) 4876.

Welsh Industrial and Maritime Museum, Bute Street, Cardiff, South Glamorgan. Telephone: Cardiff (0222) 481919.

Windermere Steamboat Museum, Rayrigg Road, Windermere, Cumbria LA23 1BN. Telephone: Windermere (096 62) 5565.

Wool House Maritime Museum, Bugle Street, Southampton, Hampshire. Telephone: Southampton (0703) 23855 or 23941.